JEWELRY MAKING

FOR FUN!

by Robin Koontz

Content Adviser: Loretta Fontaine, Loretta Fontaine Jewelry, Albany, New York
Reading Adviser: Frances J. Bonacci, Ed.D, Reading Specialist, Cambridge, Massachusetts

Compass Point Books ✦ Minneapolis, Minnesota

Compass Point Books
3109 West 50th Street, #115
Minneapolis, MN 55410

Visit Compass Point Books on the Internet at www.compasspointbooks.com
or e-mail your request to custserv@compasspointbooks.com

Editors: Lionel Bender and Brenda Haugen
Designer: Bill SMITH STUDIO
Page Production: Ben White and Ashlee Schultz
Photo Researchers: Suzanne O'Farrell and Kim Richardson
Art Director: Jaime Martens
Creative Director: Keith Griffin
Editorial Director: Nick Healy
Managing Editor: Catherine Neitge
Jewelry Making for Fun! was produced for Compass Point Books by Bender Richardson White, UK

Library of Congress Cataloging-in-Publication Data
Koontz, Robin Michal.
  Jewelry making for fun! / by Robin Koontz.
     p. cm. — (For fun)
  ISBN-13: 978-0-7565-3273-4 (library binding)
  ISBN-10: 0-7565-3273-6 (library binding)
1. Jewelry making—Juvenile literature. I. Title. II. Series.
  TT212.K66 2007
  745.594'2—dc22   2007004895

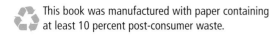
This book was manufactured with paper containing at least 10 percent post-consumer waste.

Table of Contents

The Basics

INTRODUCTION / Looking Good 4

HISTORY / Hidden Treasures. 6

GATHERING MATERIALS / Found Items. 8

JEWELRY WITH A PURPOSE / Pretty and Useful 10

WHAT YOU WILL NEED / Tools for the Job. 12

JEWELRY BASICS / Tips, Tricks, and Safety 14

GETTING STARTED / Basic Techniques 16

Doing It

SAFETY AND ORGANIZATION / Your Space 18

JEWELRY PROJECT #1 / A Friendship Bracelet 20

JEWELRY PROJECT #2 / Floral Necklace. 22

JEWELRY PROJECT #3 / A Recycled Brooch 24

JEWELRY PROJECT #4 / A Bracelet from Paper 26

JEWELRY PROJECT #5 / Wire Wrapping 28

JEWELRY PROJECT #6 / A Paper Bead Necklace 30

JEWELRY PROJECT #7 / Make and Bake Jewelry 32

People, Places, and Fun

ADORNED CELEBS / Famous Wearers 34

UNUSUAL JEWELRY / Strange but Beautiful 36

CAREERS IN JEWELRY MAKING / Jewelry Jobs 38

FAMOUS JEWELERS / The Fab Four 40

TIMELINE / What Happened When?. 42

TRIVIA / Fun Jewelry Facts. 44

● ●

QUICK REFERENCE GUIDE / Jewelry Making Words to Know. . . 46

GLOSSARY / Other Words to Know 47

WHERE TO LEARN MORE 47

INDEX 48

Note: In this book, there are two kinds of vocabulary words. Jewelry Making Words to Know are words specific to jewelry making. They are defined on page 46. Other Words to Know are helpful words that aren't related only to jewelry making. They are defined on page 47.

Looking Good

What's in your jewelry box? You probably have all kinds of trinkets that you bought or received as gifts. You can wear hairpins, tiaras, earrings, chokers, and necklaces on your head and neck. Your arms can sport armlets, bracelets, and cuff links. You can wear rings on every finger, and thumbs, too! There is room all over your clothes for brooches and buckles. Your legs and feet can be adorned with anklets, thigh bands, and toe rings. You can braid your hair in beads and ribbon. Your jewelry, and how you wear it, makes you look more interesting and lets you stand out from the crowd.

Jewelry makes you or your clothes look more attractive and eye-catching. It is sometimes used as money or to show military rank or membership in a club. Jewelry is also helpful to fasten clothing.

Jewelry Designers

Jewelry makers design and create all kinds of jewelry. Why not make your own? This book will tell you how. Your creations can be your own special signature that the world can admire.

Hidden Treasures

The first jewelry was made with things people collected. Early artists used seeds, berries, shells, pebbles, and pieces of wood that they found. They also used parts of animals such as horns, bones, claws, feathers, and even teeth.

The tomb of the ancient Egyptian boy king Tutankhamen contained some of the most spectacular jewelry ever found. The collection is probably the biggest of its kind in the world.

Near the ocean, people used coral and shells from the sea and pebbles on the beach that were polished by waves. Fossilized wood, called jet, was carved into medallions. Million-year-old tree resin, or amber, was used for beads and pendants. People learned to drill and carve other materials to make beads. Beads are one of the most common items found in early villages.

Later artists learned how to work with metals. They hammered out thin sheets of gold and cut out shapes. They also used tools to carve and punch patterns in gold pieces.

In rocky areas, artists discovered veins of blue and green turquoise streaming through the rock beneath their feet. Gold flecks sparkled in valleys and river basins. Gems shone in rocks and caves. The world was an exciting place for a jewelry maker!

Traveling Jewels

As people traveled and met people of other cultures, they traded their gems and their ideas. Jewelry making changed and evolved as civilizations grew and spread.

Rhinestones

Rhinestones, bits of quartz crystal, are named for the Rhine River in Germany where they were found. Today the word refers to glass cut into shapes to look like diamonds.

Found Items

Where can you find materials to make jewelry? Look in woods, parks, and gardens for items such as acorns, pinecones, bird feathers, and other natural debris. Gravel will have bits of quartz and other pretty fragments in the mix. Wherever you walk, keep your eyes and mind open. Take a cloth bag to gather your finds, and wear gloves to protect your hands. Think about how you might use your found items later.

Yard and garage sales, thrift stores, and second-hand stores almost always have jewelry and potential jewelry items. A piece of jewelry can be pulled apart and used again to make something new. Swap items with friends to get a great variety of materials for jewelry making. Be creative and inventive.

Painted Pasta Jewelry

All sorts of things can be made into jewelry, from nuts and bolts to small pebbles. Try gluing painted pasta shapes onto a card backing to make a necklace or pendant.

Household Jewels

Around your home you can probably find the things you will need to complete the projects in this book, such as dried pasta, needles, old newspapers, dental floss, masking tape, and glue. You might also have gift wrap and old greeting cards that you can use for paper beads. Ask your parent or guardian about these and other things such as unwanted jewelry you can use to create new pieces.

Pretty and Useful

Jewelry can be much more than just pretty. It can do a job, too. Before buttons, people used brooches to hold together their clothes. Now buttons and clasps do the job, but these can be beautiful as well as useful. Gemstone hair clips and gold combs sparkle while they hold your hair in place.

Have a look in your closet. Have you outgrown that jacket, shirt, or dress? Maybe you don't like one of your necklaces any more? Don't toss them aside. Decorate them or recycle their parts to make something beautiful and maybe useful! Colorful cloth strips make a good base for a scarf or sash. You could even make your own ornate shoelaces. Neglected necklaces and bracelets could be wristwatch bands. You can decorate old belts and buckles to make terrific jewelry that's useful, too. Your belts and buckles can sparkle with gems or metal studs or can be made from chain or strung beads.

Jewelry in Religion

Pendants can be crosses, religious figures, or other signs of faith. Rows of beads represent a cycle of prayers. And rings have long been used as symbols of love and marriage.

Jewelry in Military Forces

Jewelry is important in armies, navies, and air forces. Soldiers, sailors, and aircrew wear decorated badges and embroidered stripes that show their ranks. Medals honor their achievements.

Tools for the Job

Here are some basic tools that you will need to complete the projects in this book. You can buy them at craft and hardware stores.

Glue gun or glue stick: Glue guns use a stick of glue and heat to melt it. Glue sticks are inexpensive and easy to use.

Scissors: Scissors should be sharp so be extra careful. Don't use them to cut wire or other hard objects.

Sewing or beading needles: The hole in the needle needs to be big enough to thread the material you are using.

A jeweler at work

Safety glasses: Wear these to protect your eyes while you work.

Acrylic roller: This is a type of rolling pin with a smooth surface so it will roll out clay without sticking to it.

Straight edge and pencil: A ruler, length of wood, or heavy cardboard with a neat edge will work for tracing straight lines.

Tips, Tricks, and Safety

Threading tips: If your thread or string has a messy end, wet the end, and roll it between your fingers. Use glue to stop an end from fraying. Ribbon can be rolled and taped at the end to make it easier to thread.

Knowing knots: Use a square knot on either side of a bead to keep it from sliding. Or use a knot to separate a pendant from beads. (See pages 16-17.)

Fasteners: These must be secure and easy to open and close. Use a larger clasp for heavier jewelry. When you glue a pin to the back of a brooch, let it dry overnight before you wear it.

Using Pliers

To bend wire, hold it firmly in the jaws of the pliers. Press the wire as close to the jaws as possible, making a bend. Release, and grab the next part you want to work with. You can wrap wire around a pencil or toothpick to make loops and spirals.

Wire Wary

Wire has sharp ends. Tuck them in so they can't prick your skin or clothes. When you cut wire, wear safety glasses and make sure both ends are secure before cutting.

Basic Techniques

Knots will keep beads and other items from falling off the ends of your strands. To make a secure knot, first bring the end of the strand over to form a loop. Push the end through the loop and out. Then pull the end tight. Loop a second time on the first knot to make a double knot. There are other types of knots, including a "granny" knot, which easily comes undone. Search on the Internet for details of this and other knots.

Using beading needles: These come in lots of sizes. Pick the needle that has an eye big enough for your strand and a body small enough to thread through your beads. Use needles carefully so you don't prick yourself.

Finishing Off

Some necklaces and bracelets are made with elastic cord so you can take them off easily. Others have two ends that can be finished off with any type of clasp or fastener. Most clasps can be attached by threading the strand ends through the clasp ends and tying double knots. There are also crimps and end caps. Use your pliers to smash the crimp or end cap over the end strand after it is threaded through the clasp parts.

Using Pin-backs

These just need a little glue to attach to a brooch. Turn your brooch over. Put a dab of glue on the center of the back. Place the pin-back, pin side out, in the glue. Smear the pin-back around a bit to spread the glue. Then leave it overnight to dry.

Your Space

You have probably collected a lot of things for jewelry making. Put the items where you can easily find them. Small things can be stored in egg cartons or little boxes. For bigger items, transparent plastic bags are good because you can easily see what's inside.

Sort items by color, and make labels out of strips of masking tape. Stick the tape on the container, and write the name of what's inside with a pen or felt marker. The bags or boxes can sit on a bookshelf or fit into a shoebox. Plastic containers or jars with lids are good for storage, too. Storage bowls need to be kept where they won't spill.

Jewelry making can be messy! Even if your project doesn't need glue, needles, or paint, bits can fall on the floor and be lost or stepped on. Wear shoes, and if you are working in a room with a carpet, cover the carpet with a plastic sheet.

Create a space that is just for your projects, perhaps in the garage or workshop. Ask a parent or guardian to help. Set up a table. Surround yourself with your materials. You will also need an old sheet or blanket to spread out on the table before starting.

When you're ready to clean up, gather all your leftovers and recyclables, and then carefully shake the sheet or blanket into a garbage bag. If you have a space that you can leave, cover it up so that dust or pets can't mess up your projects.

A Friendship Bracelet

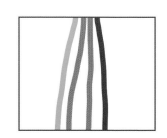

1. For the strands, use string, yarn, ribbon, and/or twine 30 inches (75 centimeters) long. Fold two lengths in half. You will be working with the loose ends. Secure the folded ends so that you can pull the loose ends tight.

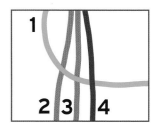

2. Keep the four loose ends flat and think of them as 1, 2, 3, and 4 from left to right. With paints, color the ends differently so you can tell them apart.

3. Cross 1 over 2 and 3, and under 4. Bring 4 under 2 and 3, and up through the loop between 1 and 2. Tighten up close to the folded ends.

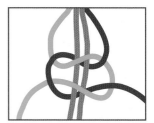

4. One is now on the right and 4 is on the left. Cross 4 under 2 and 3, and over 1. Bring 1 over 2 and 3, then down through the loop between 4 and 2. Tighten into a knot. Repeat steps 3 and 4 until you reach the desired length.

5. You can add beads at any time. String them on any of the strands. It's easy to undo the knot if you want to change things.

6. When your bracelet is as long as you want it, tie the four ends in a single knot. Trim the leftover strands. The knot will slip into the loop made by the folded ends and work like a clasp. Wrap string around the folded ends until the loop and knot have a snug fit.

Hindus give bracelets to loved ones at the festival of Rasha Bandhan. The friendship bracelets are known as *rakhis*.

Materials

- 2 30-inch (75-cm) strands of string, yarn, ribbon, or twine
- 4 colors of paint
- Beads or other decorations with holes
- Scissors

Floral Necklace

Native Hawaiians made necklaces called *leis* from seeds, bones, feathers, shells, leaves, and flowers. The Maile lei was used to show peace between chiefs. Today leis are symbols of love and friendship.

1. Gather your necklace items. You can use any of the following items: 50 to 80 silk flowers (check at garage sales!), dried flowers, fresh flowers, beads, pinecones, shells, candy, feathers, or colorful fresh leaves.

2. Use dental floss or 1-inch (2.5-cm) wide ribbon as your strand. Wrap the strand around your neck to decide the length of your necklace. Add 10 inches (25 cm) extra for tying, and cut the length with scissors.

3. Put the floss or ribbon on your work table, and spread it into

a circle. Tie the ends. Place an assortment of items around the circle. Play with color and materials until you have an arrangement you like.

4. You can either thread all the materials together using the needle and dental floss or glue the items on the ribbon. When you are finished, tie the ends of the strand, and wear your new necklace!

Hint: If you use fresh flowers, your necklace may last longer if you store it in the refrigerator.

A Recycled Brooch

If you found a lot of items to use for your jewelry, this is a great project for you! Turn a batch of bits into an unusual, eye-catching brooch.

1. You can make your brooch from such items as cloth scraps, magazines, candy wrappers, wire, bottle caps, hairpins, metal washers, broken watch parts, plastic, coins, safety pins, keys, or wires.

2. Cut the cardboard in a fun shape. You can trace the bottom of a glass for a round shape or use an object such as a cookie cutter for something different.

3. When you're happy with the design, glue the pieces to the cardboard. When the piece is dry, glue the brooch to the pin-back.

4. The brooch can also be a pendant, hat decoration, or a belt-buckle adornment.

Try to use items with a lot of color.

A Bracelet From Paper

Papier-mâché has a long history. It's easy to make, long-lasting, and has endless possibilities for jewelry.

1. Cut out a wide bracelet-sized strip from the cardboard box, and roll the strip into the shape of a thin tube. Wrap the tube around your hand with 1 inch (2.5 cm) to spare. Tape it together. This is your bracelet base.

2. Mix up the glue, water, and flour in the bowl. Soak a strip of newspaper in the mixture, and then squeeze the excess between your fingers. Wrap the strip around the cardboard tube. Repeat with more strips until you have a rounded shape.

3. For an unsual design, make shapes and bumps with squished up wet newspaper.

Painted and decorated masks are often made of papier-mâché.

4. Let the bracelet dry in an airy place for about two or three days. Decorate your bracelet with paints, glitter, sequins, confetti, or beads!

Materials

- Cardboard from a cereal box or other box
- Scissors
- Masking tape
- $1/4$ cup white glue
- $1\,1/2$ cups water
- 1 cup flour
- Mixing bowl
- 50+ newspaper strips
- Tempera paint, glitter, beads, sequins, paper confetti

Wire Wrapping

Do you have a pretty pebble or an interesting foreign coin? Wrap it to be a pendant! The object for your pendant can be a shell, pebble, coin, or other item of similar size. For the necklace strand, use a thin length of leather, ribbon, chain, or similar material.

1. Scrunch up or fold a piece of aluminum foil into the shape and size of your pendant.

2. Practice making two wire wraps around the shaped foil. Try twisting the wire different ways to make sure your design will hold your object securely.

3. When you have created a design you like, draw a picture or take a photo of it. Later you can look at your drawing or photo for reference.

4. Then wrap your object in wire. Make sure there is a loop to hang it from the necklace or use a ring.

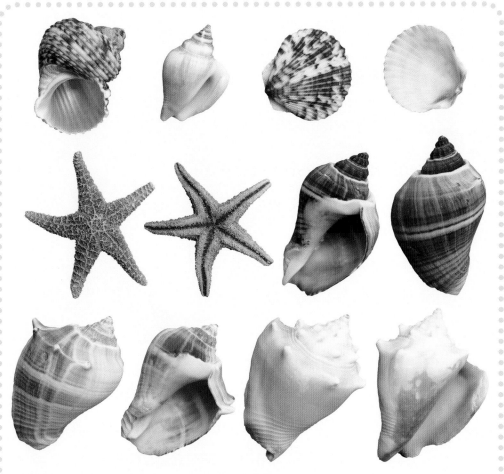

Wire Wrapping Shells

Shells make wonderful objects to wrap. Look for interesting shells next time you visit the beach. Or buy them from a selection at a store.

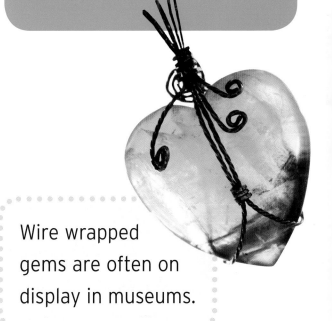

Wire wrapped gems are often on display in museums.

A Paper Bead Necklace

Paste jewelry was popular in the 17th century. Paste was made of ground glass and potash smoothed and made to look like real gems. Women would wear their paste jewelry during the day and their real gems in the evening.

Make your long, thin paste beads from paper scraps. They will look as bright and colorful as the most expensive jewelry but cost you next to nothing to make!

1. Use the pencil and ruler to map out your beads on the paper pieces. Draw strips 1 inch (2.5 cm) wide and 4 inches (10 cm) long for large beads. Cut out the strips with scissors.

2. For smaller beads, draw strips in smaller widths. For spiral beads, draw long triangle shapes.

3. Decorate plain paper strips with pens or crayons.

4. Tuck one end of a strip around a toothpick, and then start rolling it tight.

5. Spread glue on the strip as you roll, but don't get any on the toothpick. For spiral beads, start with the wide end of the strip.

6. Leave the rolled strip on the toothpick to dry. Start on your next bead. Remove the toothpicks. Using the needle, thread the paper beads onto your necklace strand.

Materials

- Paper scraps
- Felt pens, crayons, pencil, and ruler
- Scissors
- Glue stick
- Toothpicks
- Necklace strand
- Sewing or beading needle

Mix and match different color papers in your beads.

Make and Bake Jewelry

Polymer clay is a soft material that can be formed into different shapes and fired in a regular oven. It comes in lots of colors and makes fabulous beads, earrings, charms, and pendants.

Colorful Beads

Beads can be made in amazing patterns and designs by mixing clays, plastics, or glass of different colors.

1. Tape wax paper to your work surface.

2. Cut off the clay you need. Work the clay until it feels soft and pliable. Roll it out like cookie dough, using the acrylic roller.

3. Use the bread knife to cut the clay into shapes. Use the toothpick to make holes for beads, earrings, and pendants. Keep unused worked clay in plastic bags.

4. Have an adult help you follow the instructions given with the clay for oven firing. You can decorate your clay shapes as you wish with paints and varnish and then thread them onto a string to make the finished necklace.

Materials

- Wax paper and masking tape
- Polymer clay in several colors
- Acrylic (plastic) roller
- Bread knife and toothpicks
- Glass baking dish
- Plastic bags
- Paint and varnish
- String

Famous Wearers

Hollywood celebrities have made many jewelry designers famous. Some people watch award ceremonies just to see what their idols are wearing. It's a fun way to see what's new and different in jewelry and fashion design. Most celebrities can afford to buy nice jewelry, but they don't have to do so. They can just borrow items for one night! By loaning their designs, jewelers get free advertising and the stars look fabulous.

People see cool new designs and race out to buy them. Jewelry designers set new trends and make money for their work. Sometimes less expensive versions are mass-marketed. Then everyone can look like a star!

Actress Gwyneth Paltrow wears beautiful earrings.

Famous Owners

Elizabeth Taylor, a famous actress, has a huge jewelry collection. Her ex-husband, the late actor Richard Burton, gave her the "Taylor-Burton diamond." It weighs 69.42 carats and now hangs from a necklace after Taylor decided it was too big for a ring! Burton also gave her *La Peregrina*, one of the world's largest pearls.

Queen Elizabeth of England (left) has thousands of jewels with a total estimated value of about $56 million.

Strange but Beautiful

Nature and fantasy were important in jewelry design during the Art Nouveau period, in the 1890s. One famous designer, René Lalique, created winged insects in his pieces. He made dragonflies, grasshoppers, and wasps using horn or enameled gold. Imaginary monsters were also popular at the time.

Mourning rings were given to members of the family when a loved one died. Mourning jewelry was also created from the hair of the person who died. In Europe, everyday jewelry made from hair was popular. Crafters wove hair into elaborate patterns to create delicate brooches and bracelets.

Exotic Jewelry

Masai people in East Africa wear many necklaces, earrings, and bracelets made from tiny colored beads. Padaung people in Thailand wear rows of brass neck rings. In some parts of India, women wear jingling bangles from their wrists to their armpits, plus earrings, chokers, necklaces, nose rings, headdresses, toe rings, and anklets with tinkling bells—all at the same time!

Some jewelry styles may seem strange to people outside the culture. Mursi women in southern Ethiopia wear large lip plates, considered a sign of beauty.

Jewelry Jobs

There are lots of jobs in jewelry making. Several colleges and technical schools have courses in the skills mentioned here.

Bench jewelers produce different kinds of jewelry. They set stones and create tailor-made pieces for their customers. They might repair damaged items and adjust rings and other jewelry pieces.

A lamp worker creates glass beads of all shapes, colors, and sizes. Lamp workers use torches to melt and shape glass around thin pieces of steel. The space made by the steel becomes the hole through the bead. Other glass artists might also fuse glass to make special forms from glass. Their pieces are called art glass.

Designers create the images that become the jewelry. They design their pieces on paper or with wax. In recent years, computer-aided design programs (CAD) help visualize the final product. CAD also makes it easier for a designer to try different options. The computer can communicate with a production machine, which then uses the design to create a model or mold.

A jeweler's workbench

Gemologists

Gemologists are experts in gems. They can tell the type, quality, and value of gemstones. They help jewelers decide the best use for a gem. They often advise on the best cut. Gemologists also value people's jewelry.

The Fab Four

Louis Comfort Tiffany (1848-1933) is considered one of the greatest of all American designers. He is best known for beautifully colored glass and enamel jewelry and other items. It was his father, Charles, who, in 1886, invented the famous Tiffany setting, which is still the standard setting used by jewelers today.

With the Tiffany setting, the stone is supported above the ring by a circle of claws. More light can reach the stone, making it more attractive.

Another Louis and his sons and grandsons made the Cartier name one of the most famous in the world of jewelry. Between 1900 and 1939, the Cartiers created unique designs for royalty, nobility, and millionaires all over the world.

Polishing Diamonds

Gabi Tolkowsky and his team are famous for faceting and polishing many famous cut diamonds, including the world's largest, the 545.67 carat Golden Jubilee.

Fabergé Eggs

Some talented jewelers have made their craft into fine art. Peter Carl Fabergé (1846-1920) progressed from designing everyday jewelry to creating fantasy objects. He is most famous for his imperial Easter eggs. These beautifully decorated creations made from gold, a mixture of jewels, and enamel were the delight of royalty throughout Europe and Asia.

What Happened When?

| 2000 B.C. | 1000 | 1 A.D. | 500 | 1300 | 1400 | 1500 |

2500 B.C. The earliest gold jewelry is found in the tombs of the Sumerians.

500-200 Greek jewelry is developed. Artists created small figures and animals out of gold.

1320s Egyptian jewelry is at its height.

1400-1600 The Renaissance inspires more lavish jewelry than ever before.

1500s New diamond-cutting techniques such as the rose cut are developed.

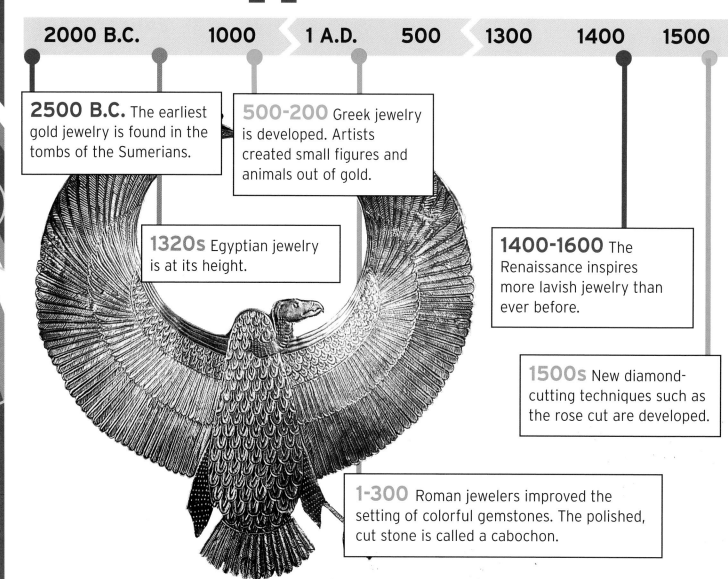

1-300 Roman jewelers improved the setting of colorful gemstones. The polished, cut stone is called a cabochon.

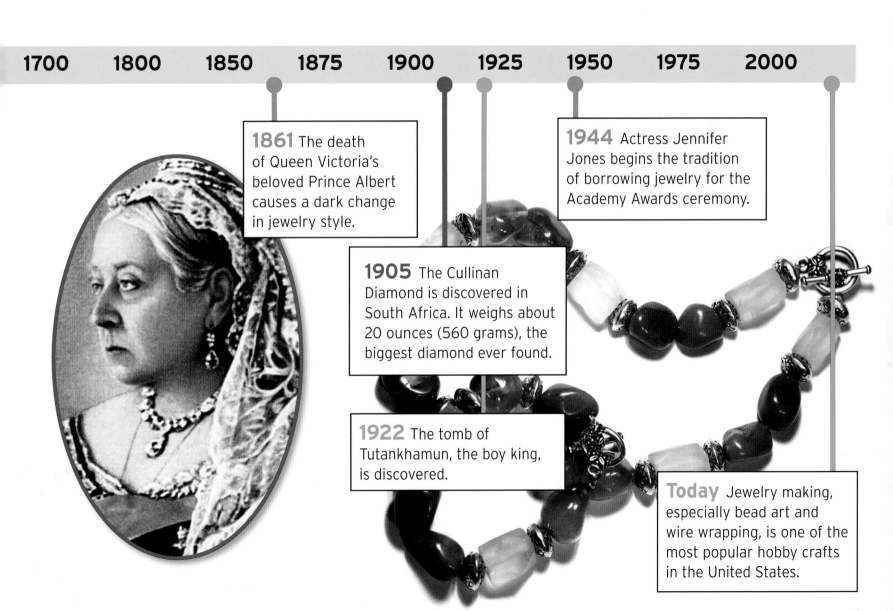

| 1700 | 1800 | 1850 | 1875 | 1900 | 1925 | 1950 | 1975 | 2000 |

1861 The death of Queen Victoria's beloved Prince Albert causes a dark change in jewelry style.

1944 Actress Jennifer Jones begins the tradition of borrowing jewelry for the Academy Awards ceremony.

1905 The Cullinan Diamond is discovered in South Africa. It weighs about 20 ounces (560 grams), the biggest diamond ever found.

1922 The tomb of Tutankhamun, the boy king, is discovered.

Today Jewelry making, especially bead art and wire wrapping, is one of the most popular hobby crafts in the United States.

Fun Jewelry Facts

A pearl is created when a grain of sand or other small fragment gets inside an oyster or mussel. The animal deposits a kind of calcium around it. In a few years, a pearl is formed.

The word jewelry comes from Latin and French words that mean joy or gladness.

Carat comes from the Greek name for a seed. The seed was used as a weight measure. When diamonds are cut, their weight is reduced.

The Hope Diamond has a dark history. Many believe the huge blue diamond is cursed. Private owners had bad luck until they passed it on. The diamond is now kept in the Smithsonian Institution.

The most expensive piece of jewelry created for a film is a necklace worn by Nicole Kidman in *Moulin Rouge*. The necklace was designed by Stefano Canturi. It was made with more than 1,300 diamonds and worth close to $1 million.

Jewelry Making Words to Know

bracelet: band that you wear around your wrist or arm

braid: wrap or intertwine three or more strands into a long, diagonally patterned ribbon

brooch: pin or a clasp that you wear on your clothing

carat: measure of the weight of precious stones; it is equal to 0.00705 ounce (0.2 g). It is also a measure of the purity of gold; pure gold is 24-carat

choker: band that you wear around your neck

Cuff links: devices that pass through buttonholes to fasten cuffs on shirtsleeves

facet: small flat surface on a gem

fastener: something that joins two items together

gemstone: mineral that can be cut or polished for jewelry

pendant: ornament that hangs down, as in a necklace

pliers: pinching tool that can hold and bend things between two jaws

polymer: chemical mix of compounds

setting: support or surrounding for a gemstone, usually on a ring

strand: any long, thin material for a bracelet, necklace, or band, such as string, twine, cord, ribbon, leather, or dental floss

tiara: decorative and often jeweled band or semicircle worn by a woman on her head

trinkets: small items or objects used as jewelry, usually of little value

turquoise: blue, blue-green, or green-gray mineral that contains copper and aluminum

twine: string that is made of two or more strands wound together

Other Words to Know

adorn: to improve the look of something by adding a beautiful object

culture: special features shared by people in a particular place or time

decorative: something that makes an object more beautiful or interesting

mourning: feeling sad or grieving for a relative or friend who has died

Navajo: American Indian people of northern New Mexico and Arizona

nobility: people who have noble or high rank in society

potash: compound that contains potassium

recyclable: can be recycled, or used again

technique: the manner in which something is done

Where to Learn More

AT THE LIBRARY

Aimone, Katherine Duncan. *The Art of Jewelry: Polymer Clay: Techniques, Projects, Inspiration.* Asheville, N.C.: Lark Books, 2006.

Jackson, Debbie. *Polymer Clay Jewelry.* Cincinnati, Ohio: North Light Books, 2004.

Sinclair, Ellsworth. *Moods in Wire.* Manassas, Va.: E. E. Sinclair, 2000.

ON THE ROAD

National Museum of Natural History 10th Street & Constitution Ave., N.W. Washington, DC 20560 202/633-1000

Millicent Rogers Museum P.O. Box A Taos, NM 87571 505/758-2462

ON THE WEB

For more information on this topic, use FactHound.

1. Go to *www.facthound.com*
2. Type in this book ID: 0756532736
3. Click on the *Fetch It* button.

FactHound will find the best Web sites for you.

INDEX

Amber, 7
Anklets, 4, 37
Armlets, 4
Art glass, 38, 40

Badges, 11
Bands, 4, 11
Bangles, 37
Beads, 4, 7, 9, 11, 14, 16, 21, 22, 27, 30, 31, 32, 33, 37, 38, 43
Belts, 11, 25
Bracelets, 4, 11, 17, 20–21, 26, 27, 36, 37
Brooches, 4, 10, 14, 17, 24–25, 36
Buckles, 4, 11, 25

Carats, 35, 40, 44
Celebrities, 34
Chokers, 4, 37
Clasps, 10, 14, 17, 21
Clay, 13, 32, 33
Clothing, 4, 10, 15
Crafters, 36
Cuff links, 4

Designers, 5, 34, 36, 39, 40–41
Diamonds, 7, 35, 40, 42, 43, 44, 45

Earrings, 4, 32, 33, 34, 37

Flowers, 22, 23

Gold, 7, 10, 36, 41, 42

Hair clips, 10

Hairpins, 4, 24

Jet, 7
Jobs, 38–39

Metals, 7, 11, 24

Necklaces, 4, 9, 10, 11, 17, 22–23, 28, 30–31, 33, 35, 37, 45
Needles, 9, 12, 16, 19, 23, 31

Papier-mâché 26–27
Pearls, 35, 44
Pebbles, 6, 7, 9, 28
Pendants, 7, 9, 11, 14, 25, 28, 29, 32, 33
Pin-backs, 17, 25

Rhinestones, 7
Ribbons, 4, 14, 20, 22, 23, 28
Rings, 4, 11, 28, 29, 29, 35, 36, 37, 38, 40

Safety, 13, 14, 15, 18–19
Shells, 6, 7, 22, 28, 29
Shoelaces, 11
Storage, 18, 19

Techniques, 16–17, 42
Tiaras, 4
Toe rings, 4, 37
Tools, 7, 12–13
Tutankhamen, 6

Wire, 12, 15, 24, 28–29, 43

ABOUT THE AUTHOR

Robin Koontz has been a freelance writer/ illustrator since 1985. She is the author and/or illustrator of many picture books, early readers, activity books and non-fiction books on a wide variety of topics. She and her husband, Marvin, live on a farm in western Oregon with two dogs and a calculating cat.